P9-CMV-748

Live a Life Worth Loving!

Copyright © 2012 by Suzy Toronto

Wonderful Wacky Women® and TingleHeart® are registered U.S. trademarks of Suzy and Al Toronto.

ISBN 0-9774956-2-0

All rights reserved. No part of this publication may be reproduced, stored in a retrieval system or transmitted in any form or by any means, electronic, mechanical, photocopying, recording or otherwise, without the written permission of the author or publisher.

Cover design and all art © 2012 by Suzy Toronto

Book design by Robert Thimm for Suzy Toronto Studios

Published by Suzy Toronto Studios, LLC, P.O. Box 265, Tangerine, FL 32777

Printed in China

First edition, 2012
Second printing. 2014

suzytoronto.com
booksarefun.com

Live a Life Worth Loving!

WRITTEN AND ILLUSTRATED BY

Suzy Toronto

Suzy Toronto Studios, LLC
Tangerine, Florida

Acknowledgments

I would like to acknowledge everyone in my world for putting up with my Drama Queen act, even when it was inconvenient to do so. I would like to thank my studio team – you know who you are – for hosing down the fires I seem to keep igniting and keeping Suzy Toronto Studios from going up in flames. My art director, Robert Thimm, manages not only to keep me organized and on task, but also has never tried to stop me when I grab a towel and head to the beach instead of to my desk. And my amazing editor, Linda Williams, cleans up my grammar, helps me stay true to my own voice, and also has mastered the unique art of throwing penguins off my iceberg.

From the bottom of my wild, wacky heart... thank you.

This book is dedicated to
Jimmie Sue Walters
and the Wonderful Wacky Women
of the Redneck Riviera

My journey has given me the opportunity to cross paths with some amazing men and women in my life. It is with great humility that I claim a wild group from Perdido Key, Florida, as my friends. They adopted my "Wonderful Wacky Women" slogan as the theme for their annual fundraiser for ovarian cancer. In just four years, this race has become a nationally recognized event, raising tens of thousands of dollars for the cause. For this group to say I inspired them is embarrassing. For they are an inspiration to me of the magnificent power of women to make a difference in the world.

Just a Quick Note from Me!

OK... so I certainly don't know it all, but I do know some things – especially when it comes to girlfriends, family, and laughing at myself. To me, these are the things that make life worth loving, and I want to share them with you. You see, I have an advanced degree from the School of Hard Knocks. And I'm not too proud to admit that I had to repeat many courses several times. I try to avoid giving unsolicited advice (especially after a kick under the table by my husband). But hey, you asked... after all, you bought this book!

Live a Life Worth Loving! has been floating around my mind for quite some time now. Since Procrastination was one of the courses I did pass with flying colors, it was easy to put the book on the back burner and let other things take priority. Yet, every so often, an unknown force would remind me that I couldn't ignore this project forever. I knew the format I wanted for the book, but the title eluded me. As I contemplated it, my husband suggested "The Art, Wit, and Wisdom of Suzy Toronto." To say I laughed hysterically at his suggestion is an understatement. Why would anybody take me seriously? Why would anyone be interested in what I had to say, much less what I thought was witty or wise? But these questions made me think more deeply about it. I have built a successful business using my art and writing, and I know many women like what I say. But do I really impart any great wisdom to the world? No. I just tell it like it is.

Then something dawned on me. The inspiration for my writing comes from ordinary, everyday women like you and me who are gutting it out through life one day at a time. You are my teachers. You inspire me to be a better person – to love more passionately, to give more freely, and to laugh more often. It's because of you that I enjoy any success at all. Maybe that's wisdom.

Women like you are also the source of my art. I believe art should be inspiring, uplifting, and empowering. Art is my legacy – I am the daughter of an artist who is the daughter of an artist. It is not an easy path to follow, but it is one filled with gratitude and an inexplicable sense of awe that what I create can touch another person's soul. When that happens, the artist is walking on hallowed ground. This is a charge that should never be taken lightly, and I believe it with all my heart and soul.

What really pushed me over the edge to finally get this book done was an encounter I had at an art show in Fort Lauderdale, Florida. A woman came into my booth and began to read my work. After a while she walked up to me. "To have written such positive, life-affirming things you surely must have led a charmed life." (I had just taken a gulp of my Diet Coke and, in a fit of irrepressible laughter, I spewed it all over myself. Not one of my more graceful moments!)

You see, "charmed" is the last word I would have used. I have been through my share of trials – supporting myself since I was 18, a premature hysterectomy in my early twenties that took away my dream of biological children, an adopted son who almost died, divorced at 29, being a single working mom, then marriage to a widower with four young children and all the joys and challenges of that situation – you know: real life. Just like you. I have struggled with both physical and emotional burdens that have pushed me to my limit – and then pushed me farther. But I would not trade those experiences for anything. They have shaped me into the woman I am today. Like my mother says, "What doesn't kill you makes you stronger."

So, in a sense, I finished this book because some hopelessly misinformed lady said I was charmed. I felt I owed it to myself and to you to write a how-to book about loving life in spite of our problems. Somewhere along the line, I want you to laugh at yourself and feel better. If that happens, I've achieved my goal.

What have I learned in the first 50 years of my life? I learned patience when I was tested more than I thought possible – and learned to laugh about it. I learned tolerance in situations that nearly broke me – and learned to laugh about that, too. I learned how to be alone and still be happy, then how to fall in love without losing myself. Now my husband and I laugh together daily. I learned to be quiet and listen to that still, small voice inside me that has never let me down. And now, while cramming chocolate into my mouth by the handful, I am still laughing. I laugh at my kids, my husband, my aging parents, my grandkids, my business, and, most of all, myself. At the end of the day, I can say that I truly have a life worth loving. I suspect you do, too.

So kick off your shoes, curl up in your favorite chair,
and join me in a laugh or two.

Welcome to my world,

Suzy

Be Wacky

We all have it in us. A free-spirited, wonderful wacky attitude
that makes our lives colorful, exciting, and fun.
It inspires us to write an upside-down,
inside-out version of our own wacky fairy tale,
filled with fascinating characters, plenty of action, and plots that twist and turn.

But sometimes we mistake that wild, unbridled energy for chaos and confusion
and allow critics to cut out the best scenes in our story.
The whole process stifles our passions and dulls our sparkle,
and we no longer fully cherish our lives.
Well, not anymore!

This is the year, and now is the moment.
Rekindle your passions, and multiply your talents.
Embrace your inner wackiness, and redefine your world.
Stand up for something worth fighting for,
and confront the dragons of the world…
especially if they scare you.
Make a difference in someone's life,
and in the process, you'll change your own.

Don't wait for "a better time." It's your life and your story.
So dare to be wacky… and truly live a life worth loving!

– Suzy Toronto

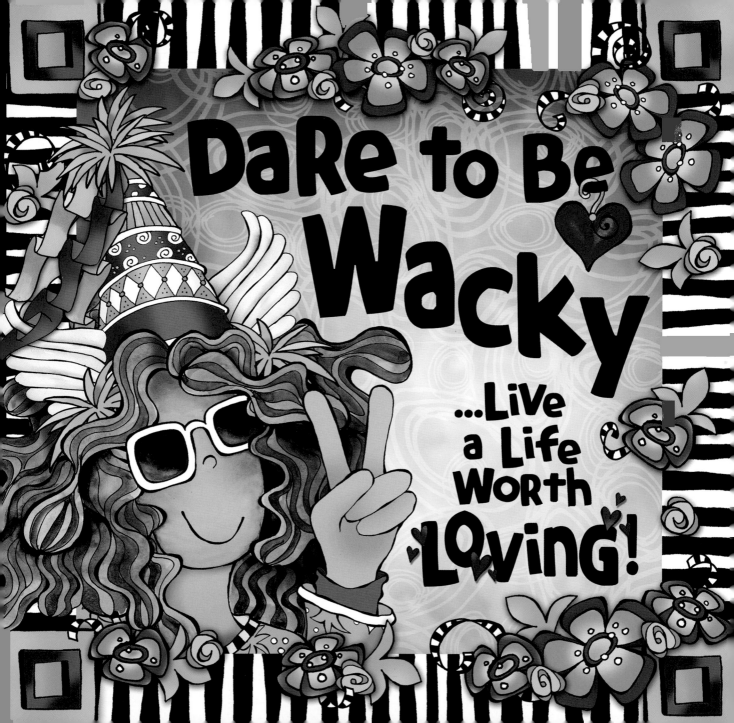

Stumble

Everyone messes up. It's part of the dance of life.
There's simply no way to avoid all the surprises along the way.
But when those obstacles become tough to negotiate,
it's inevitable that we'll stumble.
Despite the fact that the music plays on, we find ourselves
out of step and desperately searching for a "do over" button.

That's when creativity and adaptability become
our most valuable, lifesaving virtues.
They help us muster up the courage to carry on
and simply act as if it were all part of the show…
even though behind the scenes
our pride may have been battered and bruised.
Without offering apologies, excuses, or explanations,
we discover that it's just a matter of continuing onward
with all our heart and soul as if our lives depended on it.

So the next time you stumble, smile at the crowd,
kick up your heels, and dance a jig!
The moment you embrace it as your own,
no one will know it's not part of your dance.

– Suzy Toronto

Rainbows

In a perfect world,
everything would always go right.
There would be no disappointments or trials,
and life would be filled with only
sweet, warm, and fuzzy feelings.

But how would we know if things were good
if we had no comparison?
Would we recognize the blessings in our lives
without having the opposite to compare them to?
Without the darkness, would we appreciate the light?

Seems to me if we want rainbows, we gotta have rain.
The trick is to pull ourselves up by our bootstraps,
and go out and look for puddles to play in;
recognize the tempest for what it is
and train ourselves to look for the good
in every situation. By overcoming our
adversity, we find the joy in everything.
So go on, go play in the rain!

– Suzy Toronto

Chocolate

Everyone should be actively engaged
in something they truly believe in…
I believe in chocolate.
As a matter of fact,
I believe in excessive amounts
of really good, rich, dark chocolate.
Besides, I can't think of anything
that's not immoral or illegal
that makes me as happy.

And now they say it's actually good for us!
So there you go… it's a green light,
a legitimate excuse,
PERMISSION FROM GOD
to eat all the chocolate you want!

– Suzy Toronto

Behind every successful woman is a substantial amount of **chocolate**

Crazy Ideas

Some ideas sound logical right from the start.
The wheel and fire were obviously
great concepts from the get-go.

But I wonder who first watched a chicken
lay an egg and said, "Hey, let's eat that!" Yuck!
That was probably met with some skepticism.
At the time, no one had visions of fluffy chiffons,
lofty meringues, yummy omelets,
or delicate soufflés.
New ideas always encounter criticism and opposition.
But remember, most inventions begin
in somebody's basement
with one man or woman with a vision.
The key is to believe in yourself and persevere.

So trust your crazy ideas.
They could change the world!

– Suzy Toronto

Don't Let Your Frame of Mind Frame You In

Comfort Zone

Most of us spend our time neatly tucked away,
all safe and sound in our tidy little lives.
Almost without our noticing, the days start to take on a shade of gray.
It's not that we don't long for a change… it's just that sometimes
we get so busy that we forget how to really live!
Busting loose and abandoning our fears
is easier said than done. To willingly leave
the safety of our comfort zones and
reach into the fire requires a huge leap of faith.
But just on the other side, far beyond
our wildest imagination, is a magical,
mystical, uncharted territory called
"Possibility."

I'm not saying it won't be hard,
but if you keep on reaching, one of these days you'll make it…
and nothing will ever be the same again!
Because real living truly begins where your comfort zone ends,
and everything becomes possible.

So, seriously, what are you waiting for?
Life is short… if not now, when?
It's time to take that leap!

– Suzy Toronto

Beach Babes

When we tell our friends we're going to the beach,
they ask us what we do there. We look at them like they're crazy,
and very slowly we reiterate, "We… go… to… the… beach!"

For us, going to the beach is not about playing volleyball,
building sandcastles, or hauling baskets of toys, games, and food.
It's about planting ourselves in the sand with other beach babes
and proceeding to do some very serious "nothing."
It's an event… a ritual… a healing activity…
and a chance to really sit and talk.
It's about being with the girls and avoiding the sharks who so adore us.
All we need are sun, sand, and surf – along with
a few interesting people to gawk at –
and we are in our "happy place!"

So take the day off and come join us!
Then you can be a beach babe, too.

– Suzy Toronto

Girlfriends

Anyone who says she doesn't need a girlfriend
just hasn't found a good one yet.
That's not my problem... I have you.

I just can't bear the thought
of picking up the phone
and not having you on the other end
to talk to, cry to, and visit with.
You're my biggest critic, head cheerleader,
and favorite sounding board all rolled into one.

My life is infinitely more exciting,
fun, joyous, peaceful, interesting, and real
simply because you're in it.

I'm so blessed you are my friend.

– Suzy Toronto

Anyone Who Says
She Doesn't Need a Girlfriend
Just Hasn't Found a Good One Yet

Make Waves

"Now be a good girl, and don't make any waves."
That's got to be the most ridiculous statement
I have ever heard.
Not only do I plan on making waves,
I'm trying to figure out how to start a typhoon
and really rock the world.

I believe that playing "small" and timid doesn't serve anyone.
When we let our power and light fully shine from within,
we unconsciously give others permission to do the same.
And, by doing so, we get up each day
to a life that is not only worth living,
but truly worth loving as well.

So be the change the world needs.
Set the new standard. Make a difference
whenever and wherever you can.
And while you're at it…
go ahead and make some waves!

– Suzy Toronto

Dreams

You can do this! I have faith in you.
Faith in your knowledge... faith in your skills...
faith in your determination.

Keep your eye on the goal,
and don't let anything distract you.
You are in control of your destiny,
and you can make anything happen.
Believe in the power of your dreams,
and don't settle for anything less.

If you ever doubt yourself, just remember...
I believe in you. Always have, always will.
And don't ever forget it!

– Suzy Toronto

Plan B

Plan A is always my first choice.
You know, the one where
everything works out to be "happily ever after."

But more often than not, I find myself dealing with
the upside-down, inside-out version
where nothing goes as it should.
It's at this point the real test
of my character comes in...

Do I sink or do I swim?
Do I wallow in self-pity and play the victim
or simply shift gears and make the best of the situation?
The choice is mine. After all...

Life is all about
how you handle Plan B.

– Suzy Toronto

Follow Your Dreams

Do not take the advice of those
old sages and wait until you can
"walk confidently in
the direction of your dreams."
If you do, you'll never take the first step.
Instead, leap and learn to fly on the way down.
(And for heaven's sake, don't wait
until you lose ten pounds!)

Now is the time to jump in with both feet...
arms flailing, hair flying, and screaming at
the top of your lungs,
"I can do this!"

You don't have to believe it...
you just have to do it.
Start now!

– Suzy Toronto

Follow Your Dreams...

with Your Arms Flailing,
Hair Flying,
and Screaming
at the
Top of Your
Lungs!

Enjoy the Ride

Life is full of ups and downs. If you're anything like me,
more than once you've prayed to God
to take away some of the low spots.

If I had only realized that the experience
I was trying to avoid was actually
a life-altering opportunity that shaped me
into the woman I am today,
I would have yelled, "Hit me with your best shot!"

Knowing this after the fact didn't make it any easier,
but looking back I realize I am much better now
for having endured it. Besides, I'd never have realized
how high I have gotten without the perspective
of how low I had actually been.

The real lesson to be learned is that we
need to face our challenges head-on
with grace, style, and conviction.

So the next time your life starts to resemble a roller coaster,
climb into the front seat,
throw your arms in the air,
and enjoy the ride!

– Suzy Toronto

When Life Becomes a
Roller Coaster,
Climb into the Front Seat,
Throw Your Arms
in the Air,
& Enjoy the
Ride!

Age

How old are you?
Personally, at this moment,
I have no idea how old I am.
I do remember a few milestone birthdays –
you know, 18, 21, 40...
But in my head, nothing has ever changed.
I keep wondering when
everyone is going to catch on to the fact
that for the last thirty years,
I've been masquerading as an adult.

Perhaps we are, like the old saying goes,
"only as old as we feel."
In that case, I'll stay
lost in my bewilderment...
'cause really, life is what we make it,
and age is nothing
but a state of mind.

– Suzy Toronto

Pretending

William Shakespeare wrote,
"This above all: to thine ownself be true."
Boy, did he nail it on the head!

A lot of us go through phases
where we think we have to be, act, and look
like everyone else in order to fit in.
I tried it, and it didn't work.
Now I realize
God doesn't want an orchestra
of identical instruments
all playing the same tune,
so I let go of the status quo
and decided to just be me.

Besides, pretending to be a normal person
day after day is exhausting!

– Suzy Toronto

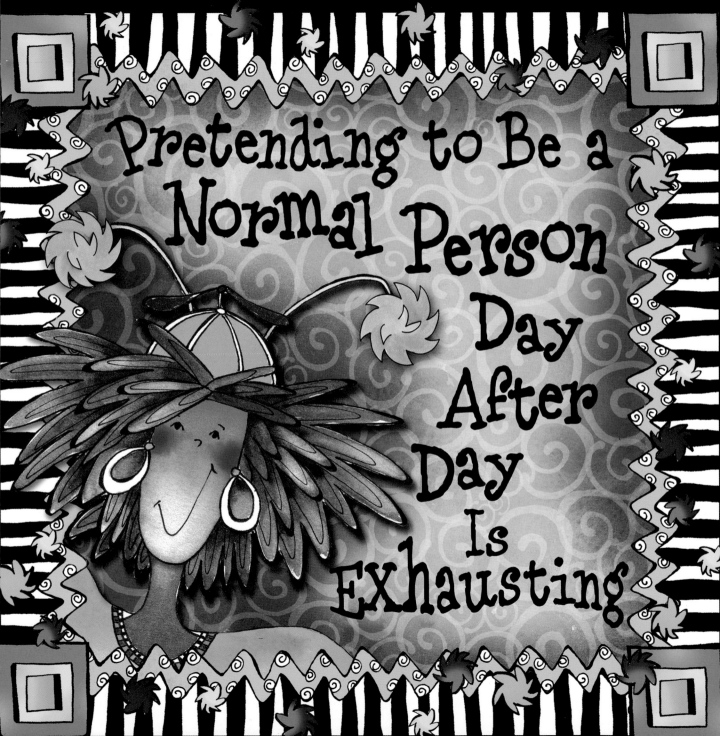

Drama Queen

More than once, someone has rolled their eyes at me,
and told me to quit being such a Drama Queen.

Instead of this stopping me in my tracks,
that one short sentence makes me want to seize
a can of spray adhesive with one hand
and a jar of glitter with the other and say,
"You're missing the whole point!" and then cover them
with a lavish coat of sticky, iridescent bling.

But instead, I take a deep breath and say a silent prayer.
I pray for the strength that I will never, ever listen
to anyone who tells me to stop being myself.
I then vow to forever embrace the drama,
to breathe in the spark of passion that lights
a fire in my soul, and to always surround myself with
the wild energy that makes my heart tingle.

You know it, I know it:
sometimes we wonderful wacky women
need to empower our inner Drama Queen
to help us create the excitement, passion, and fun
that truly make our lives worth loving…
no matter how many eyes are rolled along the way.

So stage your royal scene.
Script out your passionate performance.
And wear that crown with pride!

– Suzy Toronto

The Gathering

It is a known fact that
goddesses attract other goddesses.
You know, "Birds of a feather…"
But the really cool thing is
that quite often they flock together long before
they reach their true status of "goddess,"
giving their friendships the depth only time can give.
By the time they become goddesses,
they've been gathering together for so long –
giving, sharing, loving, and caring –
that they know intimate details about one another's lives…
making their bond unbreakable.

Whether shopping, going out to lunch, lounging over a pedicure,
or sitting on the beach, a gathering of goddesses can't be missed.
Just listen for the buzz of friendship,
the tears of shared sorrows, and the fits of irrepressible laughter.
You'll know in a minute, you're in the presence of greatness.

– Suzy Toronto

Color

As a child I was taught to always paint
the sky blue and the grass green.
I was told to be very careful
and stay inside the lines.

Why did they do that?
Life is too full of possibilities
to conform to unimportant rules that
in the end don't matter.
Rules like these stifle our creativity
and halt our progress to
achieving our full potential.

So go ahead, splash violet, melon, and chartreuse
all over your work... splatter it on the floor
if the spirit so moves you.
For now is the time to embrace your creativity.
Break the rules... and whatever you do,
don't worry about staying inside the lines.

– Suzy Toronto

Wish... Hope... Dream...

Life is full of endless possibilities.
With my brain in high gear, I can think up all kinds
of fun places to visit and things to do.
I can close my eyes and envision myself sitting
on a balmy beach, toes curled in the sand.
Or with the blink of an eye,
I can see myself skiing
down a mountain of soft, powdery snow,
living my own version of
"Rocky Mountain High."
The best thing is this: not only can I
think all these things up in my head…
if I want I can make them a reality.
The potential is within me to be and do anything
I set my mind to… and so can you.

Give it a try… wish, hope, dream…
then, with all the power you have within you,
make it happen.

– Suzy Toronto

Life Is
Too Short
to Wear
Pantyhose!

Wacky Friends

I feel blessed to have you in my life.
We are alike in so many ways,
yet different in so many others.
It seems to give a wonderful balance
to the sometimes wild wacky lives we lead.

Whether we are giggling, whining, or crying,
we always seem to have a good time doing it.
We have more fun than anyone should be allowed to
and, in the end, validate that maybe, just maybe,
our wacky lives are normal after all.

But what I really love about you are our differences.
You are strong when I am not,
level-headed when I'm feeling a bit off-balance,
and you lift me up when I think I can't go on.

And then, the icing on the cake... you put up with the very worst in me
because, deep down inside, you know the best in me is worth the hassle.

What a match we make!
Two wild wacky wonderful women riding in the front seat
of the roller coaster of life, and having the time of our lives.
I can't think of anyone I'd rather have beside me!

– Suzy Toronto

Start Living

Have you ever noticed how few people really live their lives?
They just seem to go through the motions,
always waiting for next week or next month
to give them a sense of relief.
It's a trap that's far too easy to fall into.
(Oh yeah, I know you've been there;
I was the wild-haired, wacky woman
right next to you, running around
like a chicken with her head cut off.)

So right this very second,
stop what you're doing, and start living.
Let go of the chaos and choose to
fully embrace every minute of your life.
Proclaim today as your day and this
very instant as your moment for the taking.
This day will never come again.
Next week will still come, deadlines will fly by,
and appointments will come and go,
but by tomorrow...
today will be gone forever.

So take a deep breath, let go, and LIVE!

– Suzy Toronto

"As If"...

Some days you just have to act
"as if" everything is okay, "as if" everything is normal,
and "as if" everything is just business as usual
(despite the fact that you know it's just an act).

Some people call it "fake it till you make it."
But I like to think of it more as acting with faith.
It's about believing in something you can't see or touch.
It's about reaching deeper into yourself than ever before
to find your true strength and courage...
even if they're right alongside doubt and fear.
And it's about ignoring the voices around you that tell you to give up.

Think of it this way:
What if just around the next corner
a shiny brass ring is waiting for you?
What if the rainbow's end is just around the bend,
its pot of gold emblazoned with your name?
What if you act "as if" for just one more minute?
This is not the time to wimp out and be a chicken.
This is the time to press forward with faith.
This is the time to put on your game face,
and act "as if" nothing were impossible.
When you do, you will stand tall with conviction and pride,
knowing you have finally created
the life you've always imagined.

– Suzy Toronto

Some Days You Just Have to Act "As If"...

Vacation Toes

We spend 95% of our time going through the motions of life,
longing and yearning for the 5% that's left over.
We call that 5% "vacation."

What if we could capture the concept of vacation
with something so simple as a pair of flip-flops?
We could slip them on, click our heels three times,
and in the blink of an eye, transport ourselves to a tropical isle…
or a luxury cruise ship… or an ocean boardwalk.
Women everywhere would rally in protest
and throw out their sensible pumps.
Flip-flops would become the new dress standard.

The best part is that no matter where you are,
you could wiggle your piggies,
show off your pedicure,
and turn that 5% into 100%!
Flip-flops just make your toes
feel like they're on vacation.

– Suzy Toronto

Hissie Fit

Life is all about give and take.
But some issues can't be compromised.
When the situation calls
for drastic and dramatic measures,
you have to draw a line in the sand,
climb up on a soapbox,
and protect the hill you're willing to die on.

It's not easy… anything worth fighting for never is.
But the most noble thing you can do
is stand up for what is right, no matter the cost.

The problem is your voice can drown
amid the roar of the masses.
Once in a while you have to stomp your feet,
scream at the top of your lungs,
and throw a few lightning bolts to be heard.
Never underestimate the power of a "hissie fit."

– Suzy Toronto

A Peak Life Experience

I just love a good deal, and the hunt is the best part.
None of this "buy it, bag it, take it home" stuff for me.
I don't just want a $10 dress on sale.
I want a designer gown, regularly sold for $360,
only I want it reduced to $180.
Then, with another 50% off
the lowest price marked and my
Valued-Customer discount,
I'm down to $30.

But wait, there's more!
What about that $5-off coupon
I've been carrying around for weeks
and the store credit that's tucked
in the back of my wallet?
Why, I walk away with that dress for only $10!

There is no doubt about it.
For me, finding a designer dress on a
clearance rack can truly be a peak life experience!!!

– Suzy Toronto

Only Wonderful Wacky Women
Understand That

Finding a
Designer Dress
on a
Clearance Rack
Can Be a

Peak Life
Experience

Big-Girl Panties

Yeah, I'm a big girl.
And when I need to, I can rise to any occasion.
I put on my "I-can-do-anything" face,
jump in over my head,
and learn to swim on the way up.

But don't be fooled.
I struggle just as much as anyone.
Underneath my "can-do" facade
I'm shaking in my boots,
and it's really hard to get my
sparkling and effervescent personality
to twinkle and shine!
So if I get a little testy with you,
don't take it personally.
And please… don't tell me to
put on my big-girl panties,
and deal with it.

I am wearing 'em,
but they're starting to bunch, OK!

– Suzy Toronto

Foolish Things

In our effort to masquerade
as people who really have our acts together,
goofs, blunders, and faux pas often slip out.
We get our feet stuck so far in our mouths
or our skirts flung up so high over our heads
that the spectacle is hard to miss.

This is where laughing at ourselves
becomes a lifesaving virtue.
So next time your
inner "goofball" slips out,
just throw your arms in the air,
let out a giggle, and give the world
a cross-eyed smile!

After all, we may do foolish things…
but at least we do them with enthusiasm!

– Suzy Toronto

Why Be a Queen?

There's been a lot of talk about
imitating royalty and acting like
"She Who Must Be Obeyed."

Personally, I'm getting a little weary of it all.
Maybe that's because I'm finally
past the point of being a
demanding, self-absorbed princess.
Furthermore, I've given up
the persona of the bossy queen.
Shunning all that silly sovereign hoopla,
I've simply elevated myself to the
loftiest status of all…
I am, truly, a goddess.

Besides, who wants to be a queen
when you can be a goddess?

– Suzy Toronto

Legends

We used to be ordinary women…
then one day we woke-up and
"ta-da!"… we were full-fledged,
over-the-top, head-to-toe, honest-to-goodness goddesses.
We didn't physically change on the outside, but a
magnificent transformation took place on the inside.
Looking in the mirror, we suddenly realized we were
finally at peace with everything about ourselves…
every curve of our bodies, every wave of our hair.
We now see ourselves as the sensuous
and radiant beings we truly are.

Oh yeah, there is no doubt about it.
We are legends in our own minds!

– Suzy Toronto

Think Small!

Sometimes I think big way too much.
Don't get me wrong — thinking up really big, wild and crazy ideas
is one of my favorite things to do.
But life is also about finding the simple things
that take our breath away and illuminate our tiny corner of the world.
These tender moments give our lives deeper meaning
and sometimes become our most treasured memories.
Quite simply… they make our hearts tingle.

Moments like nuzzling a newborn baby's cheek
and vowing never to forget that sweet smell.
Or sitting on a porch swing with your grandmother
and praying you'll always remember her voice.
It's laughing at a silly joke between friends
and hearing the echo of your own childhood giggles.
It's watching a parade with a lump in your throat
and your hand on your heart when the vets go by.
It's waking up in the morning and really feeling grateful for one more day.

It's easy to get caught up in the rapture
of life's brilliant, amazing, and spectacular things.
But in the end, we must always remember that life is really no big thing…
it's a zillion little things, just waiting to be cherished.
Now take a deep breath… and feel the tingle!

– Suzy Toronto

In a world where bigger is always better...

Think Small!

Work of Heart

Make your life a masterpiece.
Design it with desires and dreams.
Plan it with power and purpose.
Color it with creativity and compassion,
and forge it with family and friends.
Envelop it with energy and enthusiasm,
and wrap it all up with warmth and wonder.

If that's not your thing,
paint it with laughter,
roll it in sequins and glitter,
and string it up with a kajillion
of those little sparkly twinkle lights.
Either way, you can't go wrong.
Just make sure you do it all with love.

– Suzy Toronto

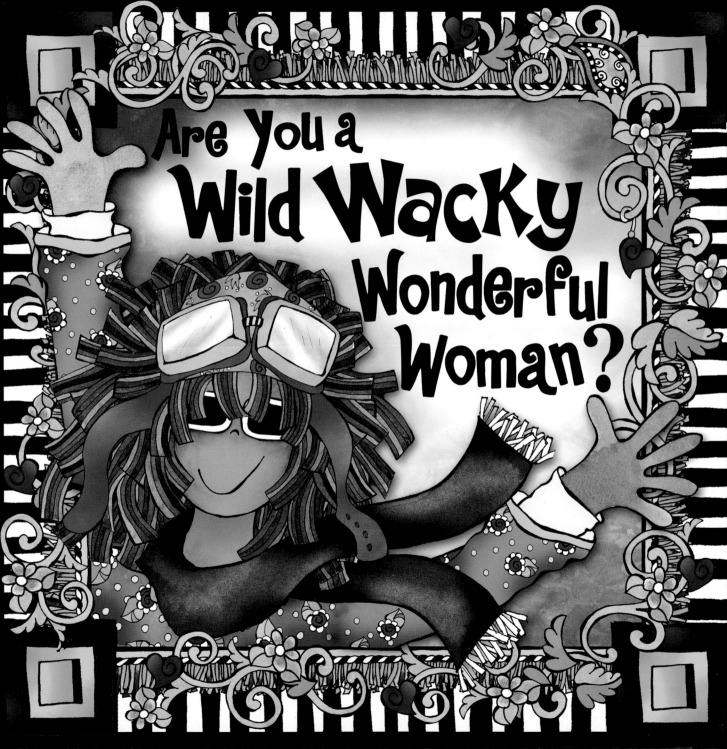

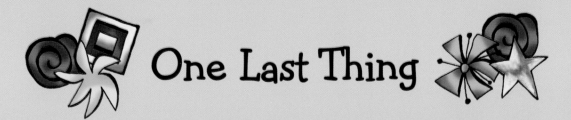# One Last Thing

I want to tell you about an incredible experience I had in college. The university I attended offered a weekly program called "The Last Lecture Series." Students would bring a brown-bag lunch, plop down on the ballroom floor of the student union center, and listen to one of the professors speak. But these men and women weren't lecturing on Shakespeare or the Russian Revolution. Nor were they there to simply share some warm and fuzzies. Their assignment was to present what could possibly be the last lecture they would ever give – basically the sum total of a life well-lived. Talk about a legacy! The series was fascinating, and I was immediately addicted. As I sat there munching on my peanut butter sandwich, I hung on every word. I was sorry when, at the end of the year, the series was over. In fact, I was heartbroken. These lectures had pushed me to see past my own little world and helped me realize what I wanted out of life. Today, over 35 years later, I look back with fondness at those days when many of the ideas, insights, and philosophies I still live by were forged on that ballroom floor.

Since this is the end of my third book, and who knows if there will be a fourth, I am inspired to share my "last lecture" with you here. So... what bit of wisdom might a wild wacky woman (who sped past the half-century mark so fast it almost gave her whiplash) have to say? Here it is – short and sweet.

Stop. Listen. Learn.

Stop. Stop churning through those endless, pointless cycles that blind you from appreciating that the world around you is so much bigger than your immediate crisis. Stop focusing inward, and look beyond yourself. Stop ignoring the rich opportunities for growth that you've passed up, simply because you call them tragedies. Stop hauling around your unnecessary baggage, whether it's emotional or physical. Unburden yourself from the constant repetition of reliving each mistake or wrong done to you. None of it serves to inspire, uplift, or empower another human being... least of all you! In short, it's self-destructive. Many women I know find themselves in a black hole just like this. But you don't have to go there... or stay there. If this sounds preachy, it is. The only reason I can get away with it is that I've done it, too. And I found that when I stopped focusing on myself, I had a multitude of time, energy, and resources to focus on making a difference in other people's lives. In the end, it changed my own and made all the difference to me. So please – just stop it. I did, and it made my life not only worth living but, more importantly, worth loving as well.

Listen. Listen to your breathing, to your heartbeat, to the sigh of your lover, to the giggle of your grandchild. Listen to the sound of the ocean, the rustle of leaves in the wind, and the silence of softly falling snow. Stop talking... and really take the time to just listen – particularly to other women. Countless women all around you have accomplished astonishing feats. Seek them out, and listen to what they have to say. Absorb all that is good in them, and let the rest drift away. Drink in the wisdom they offer. Such wisdom is everywhere, if you will just open your heart and listen.

Learn. Learn from your parents. Learn from your children. Learn from those who love you – and, even more, from those who don't. Admit that you are not always right and that you don't have all the answers. Try to look at every situation from another perspective. Learn to take a chance and make a change. Accept obstacles and challenges as opportunities to grow and become a better person. These are among our greatest gifts, but we must have the grace to accept them.

Here's the real irony of life: In order for growth to be all about you, you have to stop thinking about yourself, listen to the wisdom of those around you, and learn from it all.

See? It's easy. Just stop, listen, and learn.

May you always feel the tingle in all that life has to offer.